ZBIGNIEW HERBERT

ELEGY FOR THE DEPARTURE

and other poems

OTHER TITLES BY ZBIGNIEW HERBERT

The King of the Ants: Mythological Essays

Mr. Cogito

Still Life with a Bridle

Report from the Besieged City and Other Poems

Selected Poems

Barbarian in the Garden

ZBIGNIEW HERBERT
ELEGY FOR THE DEPARTURE
and other poems

Translated from the Polish
by John and Bogdana Carpenter

THE ECCO PRESS

THE ECCO PRESS
100 West Broad Street
Hopewell, New Jersey 08525

Published simultaneously in Canada by
Publishers Group West, Inc., Toronto, Ontario
Printed in the United States of America

Grateful acknowledgment is made to the editors of the following publications in which
these poems first appeared: *The New Yorker, The New York Review of Books, Encounter,
The Kenyon Review, Partisan Review, Salmagundi, The Paris Review, The Times Literary
Supplement, Grand Street, Parnassus, Cross Currents: A Yearbook of East European Culture,*
and *Antaeus.*

Library of Congress Cataloging-in-Publication Data
Herbert, Zbigniew.
      [Poems.   English.   Selections]
      Elegy for the departure and other poems / Zbigniew Herbert;
  translated from the Polish by John and Bogdana Carpenter.—1st ed.
          p.   cm.
      ISBN 0-88001-619-1
      1. Herbert, Zbigniew—Translations into English. I. Carpenter, John.
  II. Carpenter, Bogdana. III. Title.
PG7167.E64A23   1999
895.8'5173—dc21   98-3855
                                                                      CIP

9 8 7 6 5 4 3 2 1

FIRST EDITION 1999

CONTENTS

The translations included in this selection have not appeared in book form before. They are presented in approximate chronological order. The poems in Part I are taken from Herbert's first collection of poems, *Chord of Light* (Struna światła), which appeared in Polish in 1956. The poems in Part II come from Herbert's second and third collections of poems, *Hermes, Dog and Star* (Hermes, pies i gwiazda, 1957) and *Study of the Object* (Studium przedmiotu, 1961).

Part III comprises prose poems. They span the period from 1957 to 1969, and their order is chronological.

Part IV includes all of the poems in Herbert's volume *Elegy for the Departure* (Elegia na odejście, 1990).

I

THREE POEMS BY HEART

I
I can't find the title
of a memory about you
with a hand torn from darkness
I step on fragments of faces

soft friendly profiles
frozen into a hard contour

      circling above my head
      empty as a forehead of air
      a man's silhouette of black paper

II
living—despite
living—against
I reproach myself for the sin of forgetfulness

you left an embrace like a superfluous sweater
a look like a question

our hands won't transmit the shape of your hands
we squander them touching ordinary things

calm as a mirror
not mildewed with breath
the eyes will send back the question

every day I renew my sight
every day my touch grows
tickled by the proximity of so many things

life bubbles over like blood
Shadows gently melt
let us not allow the dead to be killed—

perhaps a cloud will transmit remembrance—
a worn profile of Roman coins

III
the women on our street
were plain and good
they patiently carried from the markets
bouquets of nourishing vegetables

the children on our street
scourge of cats

the pigeons—

        softly gray

a Poet's statue was in the park
children would roll their hoops
and colorful shouts
birds sat on the Poet's hand
read his silence

on summer evenings wives
waited patiently for lips
smelling of familiar tobacco

women could not answer
their children: will he return
when the city was setting
they put the fire out with hands
pressing their eyes

the children on our street
had a difficult death

pigeons fell lightly
like shot down air

now the lips of the Poet
form an empty horizon
birds children and wives cannot live
in the city's funereal shells
in cold eiderdowns of ashes

the city stands over water
smooth as the memory of a mirror
it reflects in the water from the bottom

and flies to a high star
where a distant fire is burning
like a page of the *Iliad*

A BALLAD THAT WE
DO NOT PERISH

Those who sailed at dawn
but will never return
left their trace on a wave—

a shell fell to the bottom of the sea
beautiful as lips turned to stone

those who walked on a sandy road
but could not reach the shuttered windows
though they already saw the roofs—

they have found shelter in a bell of air

but those who leave behind only
a room grown cold a few books
an empty inkwell white paper—

in truth they have not completely died
their whisper travels through thickets of wallpaper
their level head still lives in the ceiling

      their paradise was made of air
      of water lime and earth an angel of wind
      will pulverize the body in its hand
      they will be
      carried over the meadows of this world

THE ARDENNES FOREST

Cup your hands to scoop up sleep
as you would draw a grain of water
and the forest will come: a green cloud
a birch trunk like a chord of light
and a thousand eyelids fluttering
with forgotten leafy speech
then you will recall the white morning
when you waited for the opening of the gates

you know this land is opened by a bird
that sleeps in a tree and the tree in the earth
but here is a spring of new questions
underfoot the currents of bad roots
look at the pattern on the bark where
a chord of music tightens
the lute player who presses the frets
so the silent resounds

push away leaves: a wild strawberry
dew on a leaf the comb of grass
further a wing of a yellow damselfly
and an ant burying its sister
a wild pear sweetly ripens
above the treacheries of belladonnas
without waiting for greater rewards
sit under the tree

cup your hands to draw up memory
of the dead names dried grain
again the forest: a charred cloud
forehead branded by black light
and a thousand lids pressed
tightly on motionless eyeballs
a tree and the air broken
betrayed faith of empty shelters

that other forest is for us is for you
the dead also ask for fairy tales
for a handful of herbs water of memories
therefore by needles by rustling
and faint threads of fragrances—
no matter that a branch stops you
a shadow leads you through winding passages—
you will find and open
our Ardennes Forest

ABOUT TROY

I
Troy O Troy
an archeologist
will sift your ashes through his fingers
yet a fire occurred greater than that of the *Iliad*
for seven strings—

too few strings
one needs a chorus
a sea of laments
and thunder of mountains
rain of stone

     —how to lead
     people away from the ruins
     how to lead
     the chorus from poems—

     thinks the faultless poet
     respectably mute
     as a pillar of salt
     —The song will escape unharmed
     It escaped
     with flaming wing
     into a pure sky

The moon rises over the ruins
Troy O Troy
The city is silent

The poet struggles with his own shadow
The poet cries like a bird in the void

The moon repeats its landscape
gentle metal in smoldering ash

2
They walked along ravines of former streets
as if on a red sea of cinders

and wind lifted the red dust
faithfully painted the sunset of the city

They walked along ravines of former streets
they breathed on the frozen dawn in vain

they said: long years will pass
before the first house stands here

they walked along ravines of former streets
they thought they would find some traces

    a cripple plays
    on a harmonica
    about the braids of a willow
    about a girl

    the poet is silent
    rain falls

HOME

A home above the year's seasons
home of children animals and apples
a square of empty space
under an absent star

home was the telescope of childhood
the skin of emotion
a sister's cheek
branch of a tree

the cheek was extinguished by flame
the branch crossed out by a shell
over the powdery ash of the nest
a song of homeless infantry

home is the die of emotion
home is the cube of childhood

the wing of a burned sister

leaf of a dead tree

ARCHITECTURE

Over a delicate arch—
an eyebrow of stone—

on the unruffled forehead
of a wall

in joyful and open windows
where there are faces instead of geraniums

where rigorous rectangles
border a dreaming perspective

where a stream awakened by an ornament
flows on a quiet field of surfaces

movement meets stillness a line meets a shout
trembling uncertainty simple clarity

    you are there
    architecture
    art of fantasy and stone

    there you reside beauty
    over an arch
    light as a sigh

    on a wall
    pale from altitude

and a window
tearful with a pane of glass

a fugitive from apparent forms
I proclaim your motionless dance

CHORD

Birds leave their shadows
in their nests

leave then the lamp
instrument and book

come to a hill
where air grows

I will point out
an absent star

deep under the turf
are tender roots

small springs of clouds
beat purely

the wind will lend its mouth
for us to sing

we will knit our foreheads
not say a word

clouds have haloes
like saints

in place of eyes
we have black pebbles

good memory heals
the scar after departure

perhaps glimmers will glide
down the bent back

    truly truly I tell you
    great is the abyss
    between us
    and the light

VERSES OF A PANTHEIST

Lose me o star
—says the poet—
pierce me with the arrow of distance

spring drink me
—says the man as he drinks—
drain me to the bottom to nothingness

let the good eyes deliver me
to devouring landscapes

let words that were to protect the body
bring me an abyss

the star will strike its root in my forehead
the spring strip my face—

    then you will wake up silent
    in the hands of motionlessness
    in the heart of things

THE TROUBLES OF A LITTLE CREATOR

I

A small puppy in vast empty space
in a world not yet ready
I worked from the beginning
wearing my arm to the quick

the earth uncertain as a dandelion puffball
I pressed it with my pilgrim's foot

with a double blow of my eyes
I fixed the sky
and with a mad fantasy
imagined the color blue

I gave a shout when the image of rock
was confirmed by real touch
and I won't forget the moment when
I tore my skin on the hawthorn

in a crevice drilled by my finger
I gathered the names of plants animals
then lying in grass I admired
the shape of a fern and a peacock's tail

finally I wanted to rest
in the shadow of waves on white stone
I wrote natural history
the complete inventory of species

from a grain of salt all the way to the moon
and from the amoeba to the angel

it is for you
dear descendants
so your light dreams
aren't crushed by stones
when night devastates the world anew

2
You won't pass on your knowledge to anyone
your hearing and touch are yours alone
each one must again create
his infinity and his beginning

most difficult is to step across the abyss
opening beyond your fingernail
and to experience with your bold hand
the foreign world of lips and eyes

    —small planets are lucky
    washed by gentle blood
    blind—

    if you trust the five senses
    the world will shrink to a hazelnut

    if you believe in rushing thoughts
    you will go far into certain darkness
    on the great stilts of telescopes

this must be your fate
to be a creature with no ready shapes
who learns-forgets

it is not for you to dream of the moment
when your head will be a fixed star
you will greet not with your hand but a bundle of rays
an earth that is already extinguished

FRAGMENT OF A GREEK VASE

In the foreground you see
the handsome body of a youth

his chin leaning on the chest
a knee bent
hand like a dead branch

he has closed his eyes
renouncing even Eos

her fingers thrust into the air
her flowing hair
and the lines of her dress
form three circles of sorrow

he has closed his eyes
renouncing his copper armor

the beautiful helmet
decorated with blood and a black plume
the broken shield
and spear

he has closed his eyes
renouncing the world

leaves droop in the silent air
a branch trembles touched by a shadow of flying birds
and only the cricket hidden
in Memnon's still living hair
proclaims a convincing
praise of life

ALTAR

First came the elements: water carrying silt
earth with moist eyes quick and greedy fire
then came the gentle dragons of air shaking their manes
in this way they opened the procession for flowers and small
    plants
so the chisel of the artist of Greenness praises grass
inhuman flame like the fire thrown from ships
grass that comes when history is fulfilled
and is the chapter of silence

the tramp of sacrificial animals says good-bye
they go carnal and bright carrying warmth on their necks
and ignorance of fate on foreheads marked with horns
they fall on their foreknees very surprised at their own blood
The elements the animals shout to you the road is open
the sky parts before you and God speaks with thunder
man wretched and powerless worthy of contempt
though carried high on the back of earthly species

here there is a break in the bas-relief—if you can guess
perhaps the offering wasn't liked by the eternal gods
or the reluctant moisture of duration removed the human
    forms

a sandal and piece of a foot the goddess of Irony protected
    them
also the folds of a garment where it is easy to read
the gesture of arms beautifully raised and really that is all

you don't know which of your words and what form perhaps
    insignificant
the wrinkle of stone preserves—not what you secretly think
and you don't know whether they choose blood and bones
    perhaps an eyebrow
lying kindly in the earth where images ripen

II

FURNISHED ROOM

The room has three suitcases
a bed not mine
a closet with a mildewed mirror

when I open the door
the furniture stands still
a familiar smell envelops me
sweat sleeplessness and linen

one picture on a wall
represents Vesuvius
with a plume of smoke

I have never seen Vesuvius
I don't believe in active volcanoes

the second painting
is of a Dutch interior

from shadow
a woman's arms
incline a pitcher
a braid of milk trickles down

on the table a knife a cloth
bread a fish a bunch of onions

following the golden light
we climb three steps
through a door left ajar
the square of a garden can be seen

leaves breathe light
birds sustain the sweetness of the day

an unreal world
warm as bread
golden as an apple

peeling wallpaper
untamed furniture
cataracts over mirrors on the walls
these are the true interiors

in my room
with three suitcases
the day vanishes
into a puddle of sleep

WHAT OUR DEAD DO

Jan came this morning
—I dreamt of my father
he says

he was riding in an oak coffin
I walked next to the hearse
and father turned to me:

you dressed me nicely
and the funeral is very beautiful
at this time of year so many flowers
it must have cost a lot

don't worry about it father
—I say—let people see
we loved you
that we spared nothing

      six men in black livery
      walk nicely at our sides

father thought for a while
and said—the key to the desk
is in the silver inkwell
there is still some money
in the second drawer on the left

with this money—I say—
we will buy you a gravestone
a large one of black marble

it isn't necessary—says father—
better give it to the poor

     six men in black livery
     walk nicely at our sides
     they carry burning lanterns

again he seemed to be thinking
—take care of the flowers in the garden
cover them for the winter
I don't want them to be wasted

you are the oldest—he says—
from a little felt bag behind the painting
take out the cuff links with real pearls
let them bring you luck
my mother gave them to me
when I finished high school
then he didn't say anything
he must have entered a deeper sleep

this is how our dead
look after us
they warn us through dreams
bring back lost money
hunt for jobs
whisper the numbers of lottery tickets

or when they can't do this
knock with their fingers on the windows

and out of gratitude
we imagine immortality for them
snug as the burrow of a mouse

MY CITY

The ocean composes
on the bottom a star of salt
the air distills
shining stones
crippled memory creates
the plan of the city

starfish of streets
planets of faraway squares
green nebulae of gardens

      émigrés in their crumpled caps
      complain of the loss of substance

      treasuries with a hole at the bottom
      lose precious stones

            I dreamt I was going
            from my parents' house to school
            after all I know which way to go

            on the left the store of Paszanda
            High School Number 3 bookstores
            one can even see the head of old Bodek
            through the window

            I want to turn toward the cathedral
            suddenly the view is broken off
            there is no continuation

one simply can't go any further
yet I know very well
this is not a dead-end street

the ocean of moving memory
washes away crumbles the images

in the end the stone
on which I was born will remain

every night
I stand barefoot
before the slammed gate
of my city

BALCONIES

Balconies I am not a shepherd
a myrtle grove stream and clouds are not for me
banished Arcadian only balconies remain
I must look at the roofs as if they were open sea
where a long complaint of sinking ships is smoking

what is left for me what the cry of mandolins
a short flight and fall to the stony bottom
where one waits among gaping spectators for the tide of
    eternity
giving in return a bit of blood

this I not what I was waiting for no it isn't youth
to stand with the head in bandages and clasp one's hands
saying foolish heart bird that is shot
stay here at the precipice sweet peas
and nasturtiums are in the green box

the evening wind comes from trimmed gardens
a sea breeze with dandruff on its collar a lame storm
plaster sifts onto the deck a balcony's deck
my head in plaster a remnant of rope like a wisp of hair
I stand in the stony seriousness of senile elements

yes O clock yes my poison this will be the only journey
a journey by ferry to the other bank of the river
there is no shadow of the sea no shadow of islands
only shadows of those who are dear to us

yes only a journey by ferry only a ferry at the end
O balconies what pain the beggars are singing at the bottom
and their lamentation is joined by a voice
a voice of reconciliation before the journey by ferry

       —forgive me I did not love you enough
       I wasted my youth looking for real gardens
       and real islands in the waves' thunder

SONG OF THE DRUM

The shepherds' flutes have gone
the gold of Sunday trumpets
green echoes French horns
and violins have departed as well—

    only the drum remained
    and the drum continues to play for us
    festive marches funeral marches
    simple feelings walk
    to a beat on stiff legs
    the drummer plays
    and thought is one and one is the word
    when the drum summons the steep abyss

    we carry wheat sheaves or a tombstone
    whatever the wise drum foretells
    when the step strikes the pavement's skin
    our step so proud that shall transform the world
    to a single march a single shout

at last all men are walking
at last each one has fallen into step
a calfskin and two sticks
have broken towers and solitude
and silence is trampled
and death does not frighten when we are a crowd

above the parade a column of dust
the obedient sea will part

we'll descend to its depths
to empty hells and also higher up
we'll check the falseness of heaven
and free from fear
the whole parade will change to sand
carried by a jeering wind

so the last echo will pass
over the rebellious mildew of the earth
leaving just the drum the drum
dictator of defeated music

A SMALL BIRD

O tree spreading like the tree of the species
meant for us birds as a green house
under the held breath of spinning spheres
in sand and clay in clay and sand
in the midst of deserts where a loving wind
brings only dry rain of ashes

how can we live anywhere else but in this one tree
where we hear thick drops of falling bees
and the pitcher full of leaves is humming

a small bird I know my place I do
chained to a branch I would like to be a leaf
the smallest trembling leaf

    —because the one who abandons the tree will perish
    says the wise snake who lives in the tree
    winds round the tree and rules the tree
    he will die from thirst and hunger and fear of himself
    even if he gives flight the beautiful name of freedom

    I tell you truly says the wise snake
    if you are not obedient like the leaves
    as humble weak and docile to winds
    you will perish and all traces of you will perish—

a small bird I know my value I do
I am not like the cricket who sits under a stone
free light-hearted because all he has is a shell

soon to be left behind—an empty monument
for we have history and ruins of nests
and houses wisely lined with down
and a school of singing we are certain
will outlast the mute unmusical swarms of stars
—when a bird dies a hole in the sky suddenly opens
and gray dust pours on the greenness of the earth—

*

the sacrifice of wings hurts at first
and you can sing about this pain
then you come to love immobility
and fear composes the song's words

delaying a verdict with song
obedient to the instinct of life
we hide a spark of rebellion deep inside
when we praise sweet violence

    long odes come through the narrow throat
    the throat surely bursts from this

    and the heart bursts when the still eyes
    are brought too close

    you who read a book under the tree
    and are a bird among people

    the quill of this pen is for you—
    if you can write an elegy for my decease

with the pen preserve the colors
of fear love and despair
perhaps you will write with it a poem
about the fate of birds in cruel times

THORNS AND ROSES

Radiant and white
Saint Ignatius
passed near a rose
and threw himself onto the bush
injuring his body

with the bell of his black habit
he wanted to extinguish
the world's beauty
that sprang from the earth as if from a wound

and when he lay at the bottom
of the cradle of thorns
he saw
that the blood trickling down his forehead
congealed on his eyelashes
in the shape of a rose

and the blind hand
groping for the thorns
was pierced
by the sweet touch of petals

the cheated saint wept
in the mockery of flowers

thorns and roses
roses and thorns
we search happiness

CHOSEN BY THE STARS

It is not an angel
it is a poet

he has no wings
only a right hand
covered by feathers

he beats the air with his hand
flies up three inches
and immediately falls again

when he has fallen all the way
he kicks with his legs
hangs for a moment
waving his feathered hand

oh if he could break from the gravity of clay
he would dwell in the stars' nest
he would leap from ray to ray
he would—

but at the thought
they would be the earth for him
the stars
fall down in fright

the poet shades his eyes
with his feathered hand

he no longer dreams of flight
but of a fall
that draws like lightning
a profile of infinity

AN ANSWER

This will be a night in deep snow
which has the power to muffle steps
in deep shadow transforming
bodies to two puddles of darkness
we lie holding our breath
and even the slightest whisper of thought

if we are not tracked down by wolves
and the man in a Russian sheepskin who swings
quick-firing death on his chest
we must spring and run
in the clapping of short dry salvos
to that other longed-for shore

the earth is the same everywhere
wisdom teaches everywhere the man
weeps with white tears
mothers rock their children
the moon rises
and builds a white house for us

this will be night after hard reality
a conspiracy of the imagination
it has a taste of bread and lightness of vodka
but the choice to remain here
is confirmed by every dream about palm trees

the dream is interrupted suddenly by the arrival of three
tall men of rubber and iron

they will check your name your fear
order you to go downstairs
they won't allow you to take anything
but the compassionate face of the janitor

Hellenic Roman Medieval
East Indian Elizabethan Italian
perhaps above all French
a bit of Weimar and Versailles
we carry so many homelands
on the shoulders of a single earth

but the only one guarded
by the most singular number
is here where they will trample you into the ground
or with boldly ringing spade
make a large pit for your longing

HOW WE WERE INTRODUCED

—for perfidious protectors

I was playing in the street
no one paid attention to me
as I made forms out of sand
mumbling Rimbaud under my breath

once an elderly gentleman overheard it
—little boy you are a poet
just now we are organizing
a grass-roots literary movement

he stroked my dirty head
gave me a large lollypop
and even bought clothes
in the protective coloring of youth

I didn't have such a splendid suit
since first communion
short trousers and a wide
sailor's collar

black patent leather shoes with a buckle
white knee-high socks
the elderly gentleman took me by the hand
and led the way to the ball

other boys were there
also in short trousers

carefully shaven
shuffling their feet

—well boys now it's time to play
why are you standing in the corners
asked the elderly gentleman
—make a circle holding hands

but we didn't want tag
or blindman's buff
we had enough of the elderly gentleman
we were very hungry

so we were seated promptly
around a large table
given lemonade
and pieces of cake

now disguised as adults
with deep voices
the boys got up they praised us
or slapped us on our hands

we didn't hear anything
didn't feel anything
staring with great eyes
at the piece of cake
that kept melting
in our hot hands
and this sweet taste the first in our lives
disappeared inside our dark sleeves

IN A STUDIO

With a light step
he crosses
from one color to another
from one fruit to another

a good gardener
he holds up a flower with a stake
a man with happiness
the sun with blue

after that
he straightens his glasses
and sets tea
mutters
strokes the cat

when the Lord built the world
he furrowed his brow
calculated calculated calculated
that is why the world is perfect
and uninhabitable

instead
the world of the painter
is good
and full of mistakes
the eye wanders
from one color to another
one fruit to another

the eye mumbles
the eye smiles
remembers

the eye says it is bearable
only if one could
enter inside
there where the painter was
without wings
in slippers that fall off
without Virgil
with a cat in the pocket
a benevolent fantasy
and a hand
that unknowingly
corrects the world

A BOX CALLED THE IMAGINATION

Knock on a wall with your knuckle—
from the piece of oak
a cuckoo
will jump out

it calls forth trees
one and another
until a forest
is standing

whistle lightly—
a river will flow
a powerful thread
binding mountains with valleys

make a sound—
here is the city
with one tower
a jagged wall
and yellow houses
like dice

now
close your eyes
snow will fall
will extinguish
the green flickers of trees
the red tower

under the snow
it is night
with a clock shining at the top
the owl of the landscape

*   *   *

We fall asleep on words
we wake among words

sometimes they are gentle
simple nouns
a forest a ship

they tear themselves from us
the forest goes quickly
behind the line of the horizon

the ship sails away
without a trace or a reason

dangerous are the words
which have fallen from a whole
fragments of sentences maxims
the beginning of a refrain
of a forgotten hymn

"saved will be those who . . ."
"remember to . . ."
or "like"
a small prickly pin
that connected
the most beautiful
lost metaphor of the world

one must dream patiently
hoping the content will become complete
that the missing words
will enter their crippled sentences
and the certainty we wait for
will cast anchor

FAREWELL TO THE CITY

Chimneys salute this departure with smoke

a barge flows on the river windows quiver and complain
stucco composes a gray wreath on the pavement
the hair of dust dragging almost into infinity

on the island in a ringing of lights in black ropes
the crab of a cathedral blind dripping with soot

the stony lips of choirs
prophets' heads shells and the barking of bones
a souvenir after the psalm to a star rose and chalice

through the middle of the city with a haste of poor funerals
a barge flows on the river loaded with rubble

ON THE MARGIN OF THE TRIAL

Sanhedrin's court was not open during the night
blackness was needed by the imagination
it was in flagrant contradiction of normal practice

it is improbable
that the holiday of Passover was violated
because of a not very dangerous Galilean
the agreement of opinion of traditional antagonists—
Sadducees and Pharisees—is suspicious

it was for Caiaphas to carry out the interrogation
ius gladii was in the hands of the Romans
therefore why call on shadows
and a crowd roaring Free Barabbas

the whole affair it seems was played out between officials
pale Pilate and the tetrarch Herod
an impeccable administrative procedure
but who could ever succeed in making a drama out of this

hence the scenery of frightened bearded men
and the mob going up to a mountain named
for a skull

it might have been gray
without passions

III

BEARS

Bears are divided into brown and white, also paws, head, and trunk. They have nice snouts, and small eyes. They like greediness very much. They don't want to go to school, but sleeping in the forest—that, yes, very much. When they don't have any honey, they clutch their heads in their hands and are so sad, so sad, that I don't know. Children who love Winnie-the-Pooh would give them anything, but a hunter walks in the forest and aims with his rifle between that pair of small eyes.

A BUTTON

The best fairy tales of all are about us, how once we were small. I like most the one about how I swallowed an ivory button. My mother was crying.

CAT

He is all black, but has an electric tail. When he sleeps in the sun he is the blackest thing one can imagine. Even in his sleep he catches frightened mice. One can see this in the little claws that are growing from his paws. He is terribly nice and naughty. He picks birds off the trees before they are ripe.

COUNTRY

At the very corner of this old map is a country I long for. It is the country of apples, hills, lazy rivers, sour wine, and love. Unfortunately a huge spider has spun its web over it, and with sticky saliva has closed the toll gates of dreams.

It is always like that: an angel with a fiery sword, a spider, and conscience.

DRUNKARDS

Drunkards are people who drink at one gulp, bottoms up. But they make a face, because at the bottom they see themselves again. Through the neck of the bottle they observe faraway worlds. If they had stronger heads and more taste, they would be astronomers.

And then they set a huge table, and a magnificent wedding feast took place. That day the princess was even more beautiful than usual. Music played. Girls as lovely as moons danced below.

Well, fine, but what happened before? Oh, let's not even think about it. A black fortune-teller beats against the windows like a moth. Forty thieves lost their long knives and beards as they were fleeing, and the dragon—changed into a beetle—peacefully sleeps on an almond leaf.

—I've got you, said the wolf, and yawned. The sheep turned its teary eyes toward him. —Do you have to eat me? Is it really necessary?

—Unfortunately I must. This is how it happens in all the fables: Once upon a time a naughty sheep left its mother. In the forest it met a bad wolf who . . .

—Excuse me, this is not a forest, but my owner's farm. I did not leave my mother. I am an orphan. My mother was also eaten by a wolf.

—It doesn't matter. After your death the authors of edifying tales will look after you. They will add a background, motives, and a moral. Don't hold it against me. You have no idea how silly it is to be a bad wolf. Were it not for Aesop, we would sit on our hind legs and gaze at the sunset. I like to do this very much.

Yes, yes dear children. The wolf ate the sheep, and then licked his lips. Don't follow the wolf, dear children. Don't sacrifice yourselves for the moral.

WAR

A procession of steel roosters. Boys painted with whitewash.
Filings of aluminum destroy houses. They throw deafening balls
into the air, completely red. No one will fly away into the sky.
The earth attracts bodies and lead.

THE DEAD

Because they were closed in dark, airless chambers, their faces have become completely recast. They would like to speak, but sand has eaten away their lips. Only from time to time do they clench the air in the fist, and try clumsily to raise the head, like infants. Nothing makes them happy, neither chrysanthemums nor candles. They can't reconcile themselves to this state, the state of things.

FOREST

A path runs barefoot to the forest. Inside are many trees, a cuckoo, Hansel and Gretel, and other small animals. But there are no dwarfs, because they have left. When it gets dark an owl closes the forest with a big key, for if a cat sneaked in it would really do a lot of harm.

CROSSING GUARD

His name is 176 and he lives in a big brick with a single window. He walks out, a small altar boy of traffic, and with hands heavy as dough salutes the trains rushing by.

For many miles around: nothing. A plain with a single hump, in the middle a group of lonely trees. It isn't necessary to live here thirty years to calculate there are seven of them.

STILL LIFE

Violently separated from life, these shapes were scattered on the table with deliberate carelessness: a fish, an apple, a handful of vegetables mixed with flowers. A dead leaf of light has been added, and a bird with a bleeding head. In its petrified claws the bird clenches a small planet made of emptiness, and air taken away.

WASP

When the honey, fruit and flowery tablecloth were whisked from the table in one sweep, it flew off with a start. Entangled in the suffocating smoke of the curtains, it buzzed for a long time. At last it reached the window. It beat its weakening body repeatedly against the cold, solid air of the pane. In the last flutter of its wings drowsed the faith that the body's unrest can awaken a wind carrying us to longed-for worlds.

You who stood under the window of your beloved, who saw your happiness in a shop window—do you know how to take away the sting of this death?

A SUICIDE

He was so theatrical. He stood in front of the mirror in a black suit, a flower in his buttonhole. He put the instrument in his mouth, waited for the barrel to become warm, and smiling distractedly at his reflection—fired.

He fell like a coat thrown from the shoulders. But his soul stood for a while, shaking its head that became lighter and lighter, then reluctantly entered the body, bloody on top, at the moment when its temperature was reaching the temperature of objects. This—as is well known—foretells longevity.

He stood at the threshold of the room where his dead father was lying, wrapped like a silkworm in a silence of wax—and shouted. That's how it began.

He clung to the roar and climbed on it, higher and higher, for he knew silence means death. Rhythm of hobnailed boots, hoofbeats on a bridge—a hussar's sky-blue leggings. The thunder of drums as musketeers march into a cloud of smoke— silver sword of an officer. Roar from a cannon, the earth groaning like a drum—the triangular shako of a field marshal.

And so when he died, his faithful soldiers wanted him to ascend heaven by the ladder of tumult. A hundred bell towers rocked the town. At the moment when it swung closest to the sky, the gunners fired. But they could not split off enough of the blue glaze to slip in the field marshal, complete with his sword and triangular shako.

Now he comes loose again, and falls on the face of the earth. His faithful soldiers pick him up, and once again fire at the sky.

HOTEL

The carpet is too soft. Also the palm tree in the lobby is unbelievable. For a long time the Maitre looks at our faces, shuffling passports in his hands. "Such dark-ringed eyes, such dark-ringed eyes. I knew a merchant from Smyrna, who also had a false front tooth. Nowadays one has to be terribly careful: informers and scorpions are everywhere."

In the elevator we stand facing the mirror, but already at the first jerk we see silvery mildew in the place of our faces.

CLOCK

In appearance it is the peaceful face of a miller, full, shiny as an apple. Only a single dark hair moves on it. But when one looks inside: a nest of worms, the inside of an anthill. And this is supposed to lead us to eternity.

This autumn the trees have found peace at last. They stand all the time in a hard, somewhat spiteful greenness, without a trace of yellow or grain of red in their leaves. The grass is thick, firmly driven into the earth's skin, and in no way resembles the pelts of old animals. Untouched roses turn their hot planets around insects as motionless and skinny as moons.

Only the statues live through an autumn that is tragic because it is the last. Rotting pedestals reveal the impermanence of the builders of empires. The wings of angels and plumes of admirals are crumbling. The cracked forehead of a philosopher exposes a frightening emptiness of broken vessels. Where there was once a prophet's index finger, a small spider now floats, attached to a gossamer thread.

Gray-haired lovers walk under eternal trees on a path scattered with the crunching fingers of gods and caesars.

Once there was breath on these window panes, the fragrance of a roast, the same face in the mirror. Now it is a museum. The flora of the floors has been exterminated, the chests emptied, rooms flooded with wax. For entire days and nights they kept the windows open. Mice avoid this infected house.

The bed is neatly made. But no one wants to spend even a single night here.

Between his wardrobe, his bed and his table—the white frontier of absence, precise as the cast of a hand.

PRINCIPALITY

Designated in the guide by two stars (in reality there are more), the entire principality—the city, sea, and a piece of sky—at first glance looks wonderful. The tombs are whitewashed, the houses opulent, the flowers fat.

All the citizens are guardians of souvenirs. Because of a small inflow of tourists there is little work—an hour in the morning, an hour in the evening.

In the middle, a siesta.

Red as an eiderdown, a cloud of snoring hovers over the principality. Only the prince is not asleep. He rocks to sleep the head of the local god.

The hotels and boarding houses are occupied by angels who have taken a liking to the principality for its warm spas, serious customs, and air that is distilled by the labor of pens polishing memory.

CHINESE WALLPAPER

A deserted island with the sugary head of a volcano. In the middle of smooth water, reeds and a fisherman with a pole. Higher, an island is spread out like an apple tree with a pagoda and small bridge, where lovers meet under the blossoming moon.

If that was all, it would be a nice episode: a history of the world in a few words. But it is repeated into infinity with thoughtless, stubborn exactitude: volcano, lovers, the moon.

One cannot make a greater insult to the world.

CERNUNNOS

The new gods walked behind the Roman army at a suitable distance, so Venus's swaying hips and Bacchus's uncontrolled fits of laughter would not seem improper. Ashes were still warm, ants and beetles solemnly burying the barbarian heroes.

The old gods watched the entrance of the new ones from behind trees, without sympathy but with admiration. The white, hairless bodies seemed weak yet attractive.

Despite difficulties with language a summit meeting took place. After a few conferences, spheres of influence were divided up. The old gods were content with minor positions in the provinces. But for important ceremonies their figures were carved in stone—crumbly sandstone—together with the gods of the conquerors.

The real shadow on the collaboration was cast by Cernunnos. Although he adopted a Latin ending on the advice of his colleagues, no laurel could conceal his spreading, constantly growing horns.

This is why he usually resided in distant woods. Often he could be seen in dark meadows at dusk. In one hand he holds a serpent with a lamb's head, with the other he draws signs on the air that are completely incomprehensible.

A NATIVE DEVIL

I

He came from the West, at the beginning of the tenth century. At first he was brimming with energy and ideas. The clatter of his hooves could be heard everywhere, the air smelled of brimstone. This virginal country, closer to hell than heaven, seemed to be his promised land. The wavering soul of the people begged for a baptism of dark fire.

Belfries rocked on the hills. Monks squeaked like mice. Holy water flowed in jugfuls.

2

He leased castles and cities to masters of alchemy and quack magicians. As for himself he sank his ten claws into the healthy meat of the nation—the peasants. He would enter into the body deeply, but leave no trace. Matricides hammered together votive chapels; fallen girls raised themselves up. Those who were possessed smiled idiotically.

The muscles of the angels grew flabby. People fell into a dull virtue.

3

The odor of sulfur left him very quickly. He began to smell innocently of hay. He started to drink. He neglected himself completely. If he enters stables, he won't tie the cows' tails together. He doesn't even tease women's nipples at night.

But he will outlive everyone. As stubborn as a nettle, lazy as a weed.

IV

OAKS

In a forest on a dune three full-grown oaks
from whom I seek advice and help
because choruses are silent the prophets have departed
there is no one on the earth more
worthy of respect this is why—O oaks—
I direct dark questions to you
I wait for the verdict of fate as once at Dodona

Though I must admit—wise ones—I am troubled
by the ritual of your conception
toward spring's close the beginning of summer
in the shade of your limbs it is swarming
with your children and infants
foster homes of leaves orphanages of sprouts
pale very pale
weaker than grass
on the ocean of sand
they struggle alone alone
why don't you protect your children
whom the first frost will cut down with the sword of
    annihilation

What does this mad crusade mean—oaks—
the slaughter of innocents grim selection
this Nietzschean spirit on a dune so quiet
it might comfort the suffering of Keats's nightingale
here where everything seems inclined
to kisses confessions reconciliation

How am I to understand your dark parables
baroque of rosy angels laughter of white tibias
judgment at dawn execution at night
life groping in blindness mixed with death
let us pass over the baroque which I can't stand
but who rules
is it a watery-eyed god with the face of an accountant
a demiurge of infamous statistical tables
who plays dice that always come out in his favor
is necessity only a variant of chance
and meaning the yearning of the weak an illusion
    of the disappointed

        So many questions—O oaks—
so many leaves and under each leaf
despair

TRANSFORMATIONS OF LIVY

How did they understand Livy my grandfather my great
    grandfather
certainly they read him in high school
at the not very propitious time of year
when a chestnut stands in the window—fervent candelabras of
    blooms—
all the thoughts of grandfather and great grandfather running
    breathless to Mizia
who sings in the garden shows her décolleté also her heavenly
    legs up to the knees
or Gabi from the Vienna opera with ringlets like a cherub
Gabi with a snub nose and Mozart in her throat
or in the end to kind-hearted Józia refuge of the dejected
with no beauty talent or great demands
and so they read Livy—O season of blossoms—
in the smell of chalk boredom naphthalene for cleaning the
    floor
under a portrait of the emperor
because at that time there was an emperor
and the empire like all empires
seemed eternal

Reading the history of the City they surrendered to the illusion
that they are Romans or descendants of Romans
these sons of the conquered themselves enslaved
surely the Latin master contributed to this
with his rank of Court Councillor
a collection of antique virtues under a worn-out frock coat

so following Livy he implanted in his pupils contempt for the
    mob
the revolt of the people—*res tam foede*—aroused loathing in
    them
whereas all of the conquests appeared just
they showed simply the victory of what is better stronger
that is why they were pained by the defeat at Lake Trasimeno
the superiority of Scipio filled them with pride
they learned of the death of Hannibal with genuine relief
easily too easily they let themselves be led
through the entrenchments of subordinate clauses
complex constructions governed by the gerund
rivers swollen with elocution
pitfalls of syntax
—to battle
for a cause not theirs

Only my father and myself after him
read Livy against Livy
carefully examining what is underneath the fresco
this is why the theatrical gesture of Scevola awoke no echo
    in us
shouts of centurions triumphal marches
while we were willing to be moved by the defeat
of the Samnites Gauls or Etruscans
we counted many of the names of peoples turned to dust by the
    Romans
buried without glory who for Livy
were not worth even a wrinkle of style
those Hirpins Apuleans Lucanians Osunans
also the inhabitants of Tarentum Metapontis Locri

My father knew well and I also know
that one day on a remote boundary
without any signs in heaven
in Pannonia Sarajevo or Trebizond
in a city by a cold sea
or in a valley of Panshir
a local conflagration will explode

and the empire will fall

THE NEPENTHE FAMILY

Did Jean-Jaques the Tender know about the pitcher plant
—it was described by Linnaeus he should have known it—
so why was he silent about this scandal of nature

one of many scandals but perhaps
beyond the capacity of the heart and tear glands
of the one who sought only comfort in nature

      this criminal grows in the dark jungles of Borneo
      and lures with a flower that is not a flower
      but the main vein of a leaf fanned out in the form
         of a pitcher

      with a hinged lid and very sweet mouth
      that draws insects to the treacherous banquet
      like the secret police of a certain empire

      for who can resist—fly or man—
      the sticky nectars orgy of colors glowing with hues
      of white of violet of meat like the windows of a red tavern

      where a kind innkeeper with a beautiful daughter wife
      sends the company of drunken guests drained of blood
      to heaven or hell depending on their merits

      it was a favorite of the Victorian decadents
      combining the salon of debauchery with the
         torture chamber

everything was there—rope nails venom sex the knout
the coffin

and we live peacefully with the pitcher plant
among gulags concentration camps with no concern for the
knowledge
that innocence in the world of plants—does not exist

BLACKTHORN

In spite of the worst forecasts of the diviners of weather
—a wide wedge of polar air sunk to its hilt in sky—
in spite of the instinct for life of the sacred strategy for survival
—other plants deliberately gather strength for a leap
and mass buds on the black front lines before attack—
before Prospero raises his hand
the blackthorn begins its solo concert
in the cold empty hall

this wayside shrub shatters
the conspiracy of the cautious
and it is
like handsome young volunteers
who fall on the first day of war in brand-new uniforms
soles of their shoes barely written on by sand
like stars of poetry extinguished too early
like a field trip of children swept away by an avalanche
like those who see clearly in darkness
like insurgents who against the clocks of history
against the worst predictions
despite everything they begin

o madness of naive white blooms
blinding blizzard
crest of a wave
an aubade with a short stubborn ostinato
halo with no head

yes blackthorn
a few measures
in an empty hall
and then torn musical notes
lie among puddles and rusty weeds
so no one remembers

someone however must have courage
someone must begin

yes blackthorn
a few clear measures
it is a lot
it is everything

MASS FOR THE IMPRISONED

—for Adam Michnik

If it is an offering for those in prison
best of all let it be in an improper place

with no marble no music
gold incense whiteness

next to a clay pit under a slovenly willow
as sleet lashes

in an abandoned mine
a burned-down sawmill
or warehouse of hunger
where Angels of Judgment
do not look down from peeling walls
instead
salt
vinegar

if it is to be an offering
we must unite
with brothers in the grip of lawlessness
who fight at the extreme limit

I see
their light shadows
they move slowly
as if on the bottom of the ocean

I see
their idle hands
awkward elbows and knees
cheeks where shadow is nesting
mouths open in sleep
helpless backs

    we are here alone
    —my mystagogue—
    no others in prayer
    I watch as you speak with the goblet
    tie and untie the knot
    drop crumbs then pick them up

and I listen
above my head
to the flying
the rustling
of a gray numen

thus we continue
conspirators

among prophetic sounds
and trivial sounds

the dignified silence of bells
the obstinate barking of keys

SMALL HEART

—for Jan Józef Szczepański

The bullet that I shot
at the time of the great war
made a circle around the globe
and struck me in the back

at the least suitable moment
when I was already sure
I had forgotten everything
his-my faults

after all just like others
I wanted to erase from memory
the faces of hatred

history consoled me
that I had fought with naked force
and the Book said
—it is he who is Cain

so many years patiently
so many years in vain
with water of compassion I washed away
soot blood insults
so nobility
the beauty of existence
and perhaps even goodness
could have a home in me

after all just like everyone
I longed to return
to the bay of childhood
to the land of innocence

the bullet I shot
from a small calibre weapon
circled the globe
against the laws of gravitation
and struck me in the back
as if it wanted to say
—that nothing will be forgiven
to anyone

so now I sit alone
on the cut stump of a tree
exactly in the centre
of the forgotten battle

and I
gray spider
weave bitter meditations

about too great a memory
about too small a heart

REQUEST

Father of the gods and you Hermes my patron
I forgot to ask you—and now it is late—
for a gift as great
and shameful as a prayer
for smooth skin for thick hair almond-shaped lids

let my whole life
be completely contained
inside Countess Popescu's
casket of keepsakes
on its cover a shepherd
at the edge of an oak forest
blowing
a pearl-like air
from a pipe

while inside is disorder
a cuff link
father's old watch
a ring with its stone missing
a collapsible ship's telescope
dried-up letters
a golden inscription on a cup
inviting you to the waters
of Marienbad
a bar of sealing wax
a cambric handkerchief
the sign for surrender of a fortress

a bit of mould
a bit of fog

Father of the gods and you Hermes my patron
I forgot to ask you
for mornings noons frivolous evenings without meaning
for little soul
very little conscience
a light head

and for a dancing step

MR. COGITO'S HERALDIC MEDITATIONS

Before—perhaps an eagle
on a vast red field
and a trumpet of wind

now
made of straw
of stammering
of sand

still without a face
its eyes sealed
a puppy

neither yellow bile of hatred
nor the scarlet of fame
nor green of hope

an empty shield

across a landscape
of small trees
of small words
of crickets

a snail
winds its way

on its back
it carries its home

dark

uncertain

FAREWELL

The moment has come we have to say farewell
after the migration of birds the sudden migration of greenness
the end of summer—a banal subject for solo guitar

I live now on the slope of a hill
the entire length of the wall is a window so I see exactly
the dense fur of osiers naked willows this is my shore

everything develops in horizontal bands—the lazy river
the other high shore steeply dropping down
reveals at last what had to be admitted

clay sand limestone patches of humus
and a now meager forest a weeping forest

I am happy that is devoid of illusions
the sun appears briefly but in return gives
grandiose spectacles when it goes down somewhat in
    Nero's taste

I am calm it is time to say farewell
our bodies have put on the color of earth

LANDSCAPE

It is a windy night and an empty road where the army of
    the Prince of Parma
has left dead bodies of horses
bones of a recently captured castle shine on a bald mountain
there is only stone sand dung and wind with no aim or color

What animates the landscape is a moon sharply nailed into
    the sky
and a few dirty shadows below
also white gallows for on them the thin husks of bodies
are hanging the wind brings them back to life wind without
    trees and without clouds

A JOURNEY

I

If you set out on a journey let it be long
wandering that seems to have no aim groping your way blindly
so you learn the roughness of the earth not only with your eyes
    but by touch
so you confront the world with your whole skin

2

Befriend the Greek from Ephesus the Jew from Alexandria
they will lead you through sleeping bazaars
cities of treaties hidden entrances
there on an emerald tablet above an extinguishing *athanor*
are swaying Basileos Valens Zosima Geber Filalet
(the gold evaporated wisdom remained)
through a half-open veil of Isis
corridors like mirrors framed by darkness
silent initiations and innocent orgies
through deserted tunnels of myths and religions
you will reach the naked gods without symbols
dead that is immortal in their monsters' shadows

3

When you come to know keep your knowledge silent
learn the world anew like an Ionian philosopher
taste water and fire air and earth
because they will remain when everything passes away
and the journey will remain though no longer yours

4

Then your native land will seem small
a cradle a boat tied to a branch with your mother's hair
when you mention its name no one at the campfire
will know which mountain it lies behind
what kind of trees it bears
when really it needs so little tenderness
repeat the funny sounds of its speech before going to sleep
że—czy—się
smile at the blind icon before sleep
at burdocks at the brook the brood of chicks
home has gone
there is a cloud over the world

5

Discover the insignificance of speech the royal power of
    gesture
uselessness of concepts the purity of vowels
with which everything can be expressed sorrow joy
    rapture anger
but do not hold anger
accept everything

6

What city is this what bay what street river
the rock that grows in the sea does not ask for a name
the earth is like sky
signposts of winds lights high and low
inscriptions crumbled to dust
memories worn by sand rain and grass
names are like music transparent and with no meaning
Kalambaka Orchomenos Kavalla Levadia

the clock stops and from now on hours are black white or blue
they absorb the thought that you lose the lines of your face
what answer can an eroded inscription give to thistles
give back the empty saddle with no regret
give the air back to another

7
So if it is to be a journey let it be long
a true journey from which you do not return
the repetition of the world elementary journey
conversation with the elements question without answer
a pact forced after struggle
                         great reconciliation

WIT STWOSZ: MADONNA FALLING ASLEEP

Like tents before a storm golden cloaks ripple
a flood of hot scarlet exposes chests and feet
cedar apostles raise their huge heads
a beard dark as an axe hangs from the heights

The woodcarvers' fingers blossom. The miracle slips from their
    hands
so they put them in the air—the air becomes stormy as chords
Stars dim in the sky music also comes from the stars
but doesn't reach the earth it remains high as the moon.

And Mary falls asleep. She goes to the bottom of astonishment
loving eyes hold her in the frail net of the retina
she falls higher and higher filters through fingers like a stream
and they bend with difficulty over the mounting cloud

PRAYER OF THE OLD MEN

but later later on
won't you push us away
when the children women patient animals have left
because they can't bear wax hands

movements uncertain as the flight of a butterfly
stubborn silence and the cough of our speech
and the moment is near when the world shrinks in the eye
they will remove it from the eye like a tear and break it like
    glass
when the drawer of memory suddenly opens

I ask about it
will you then
accept us again
because it will be like a return to the lap of childhood
to a great tree to a dark room
an interrupted conversation to weeping without sorrow

I know
it is a matter of blood
and we who are lazy mystics dragging our feet
a lopsided psalm in our deformed fingers
we listen to sand pouring in our veins
and in our dark interior grows a white church
of salt memories calcium and unspeakable weakness

clinging to the taste of wafer and white cloth
they bring you in again

through the asthmatic wheezing of bells
by lit flowers

if it is difficult to make angels out of us
change us into heavenly dogs
mongrels with rumpled hair
moths with gray faces
the extinguished eyes of gravel
but don't allow us
to be devoured
by the insatiable darkness of your altars
say just one thing
that we will return later

THE ADVENTURES OF MR. COGITO WITH MUSIC

I
long ago
actually since the dawn of his life
Mr. Cogito surrendered
to the tantalizing spell of music

he was carried though the forests of infancy
by his mother's melodious voice

Ukrainian nurses
hummed him to sleep
a lullaby spread wide as the Dnieper

he grew
as if urged on by sounds
in chords
dissonances
vertiginous crescendoes

he was given a basic
musical education
not complete to be sure
a First Piano Book
(part one)

he remembers hunger as a student
more intense than the hunger for food

when he waited before a concert
for the gift of a free ticket

it is difficult to say when
he began to be tormented
by doubts
scruples
the reproach of conscience

he listened to music rarely
not voraciously as before
with a growing feeling of shame

the spring of joy had dried up

it was not the fault
of the masters
of the motet
the sonata
the fugue

the revolutions of things
fields of gravitation
had changed
and together with them
the inner axis
of Mr. Cogito

he could not
enter the river
of earlier rapture

2

Mr. Cogito
began to collect
arguments against music

as if he intended to write
a treatise on disappointed love

to drown harmony
with angry rhetoric

to cast his own burden
onto the frail shoulders of the violin

the hood of anathema
over a clear face

> but let us think about it impartially
> music
> is not without fault
>
> its inglorious beginnings—
> sounds in intervals
> drove workers on
> wrung out sweat
>
> the Etruscans flogged slaves
> to the accompaniment of pipes and flutes
>
> and therefore
> morally indifferent

like the sides of a triangle
the spiral of Archimedes
the anatomy of a bee

it abandons the three dimensions
flirts with infinity
places ephemeral ornaments
over the abyss of time

its obvious and hidden power
caused anxiety among philosophers

the godlike Plato warned—
changes in musical style
provoke social upheavals
the abolition of laws

gentle Leibniz consoled
that nevertheless it provides order
and is a hidden
arithmetic
training
of the soul

but what is it
what is it really

—a metronome of the universe
—exaltation of air
—celestial medicine
—a steam whistle of emotion

3
Mr. Cogito
suspends without answer
reflections on the essence of music

but the tyrannical power of this art
does not leave him in peace

the momentum with which it forces
its way into our interior

it makes us sad without reason
it gives us joy with no cause

it fills harelike hearts
of recruits with the blood of heroes

it absolves too easily
it purifies free of charge

—and who gave it the right
to wrench us by the hair
to wring tears from the eyes
to provoke us to attack

Mr. Cogito
who is condemned to stony speech
grating syllables
secretly adores
volatile light-mindedness

the carnival of an island and groves
beyond good and evil

the true cause of the separation
is incompatibility of character

different symmetry of the body
different orbits of conscience

Mr. Cogito
always defended himself
against the smoke of time

he valued concrete objects
standing quietly in space

he worshipped things that are permanent
almost immortal

dreams of the speech of cherubs
he left in the garden of dreams

he chose
what depends
on earthly measure and judgment

so when the hour comes
he can consent without a murmur

to the trial of truth and falsehood
to the trial of fire and water

SPECULATIONS ON THE SUBJECT OF BARABBAS

What happened to Barabbas. I ask no one knows
Released from the chain he walked out into a white street
he could turn right go straight ahead turn left
spin on his heels crow happily as a rooster
He Emperor of his own hands and head
He Governor of his own breath

I ask because in a sense I took part in the affair
Attracted by the crowd in front of Pilate's palace I shouted
like the others Barabbas let Barabbas free
Everyone shouted if I alone had been silent
it still would have happened as it was supposed to happen

Perhaps Barabbas returned to his band
In the mountains he kills quickly robs with precision
Or he opened a pottery shop
And cleans hands soiled by crimes
in the clay of creation
He is a water carrier mule driver money lender
ship owner—Paul sailed to the Corinthians on one of them

or—this can't be ruled out—
became a prized spy paid by the Romans

Look and admire the stunning game of fate
for chances of power smiles of fortune

While the Nazarene
remained alone
without an alternative
with a steep
path
of blood

WAGON

What is he doing
this hundred-year-old man
with a face like an ancient book
his eyes without tears
lips pressed
watching over the memories
and mumblings of history

now
when winter mountains
are extinguished
and Fujiyama enters the constellation of Orion
Hirohito
a hundred-year-old man—emperor god and state official—
is writing

these are not acts
of mercy
or acts of anger
nominations
of generals
ingenious tortures
but a composition
for the annual competition
of traditional poetry

the subject
is a wagon
the form: the venerable tanka

five lines
thirty-one feet

"as I get on the train
of the state railway
I think of the world
of my grandfather Emperor Meiji"

a poem
coarse in appearance
its breath held in check
with no artificial blushes

different
from shamelessly wet
modern productions
filled with triumphant howling

a crumb
about a railway
devoid of melancholy
of haste before a long journey
even
of sadness and hope

I think
with my heart tensed
about Hirohito

about his bent back
frozen head
the face of an old doll

119

I think of his
dried eyes
small hands
his thought slow
like the pause
between one owl calling
and another

I think
with my heart tensed
what will be the fate
of traditional poetry

will it depart
following the emperor's shadow
vanishing
weightless

THE DEATH OF LEV

I
With great bounds
across an immense field
under a sky heavy
with December clouds
Lev flees
from Yasnaya Polana
to the dark woods

behind him a thick
line of hunters

with great bounds
his beard streaming behind
face inspired
by the fires of anger
Lev flees like a lion
to the forest on the horizon

behind him
Lord have mercy

an unrelenting line of beaters
moves ahead
hunters beating for Lev

in front
Sofia Andreyevna
drenched completely

after the morning suicide
she lures him
—Lovochka
in a voice
that could shatter stones

behind her
sons daughters
servants hangers-on
policemen Orthodox priests
bluestockings
moderates anarchists
Christians illiterates
Tolstoyans
Cossacks
and every possible kind of riffraff

old women squeal
peasants bellow

hell

2

the finale
at the small station of Astapovo
a wooden knocker
near the railway

a merciful train worker
put Lev in bed

now he is safe

above the small station
the lights of history go on

Lev closes his eyes
no longer curious about the world

only the bold
priest Pimen
who has vowed
he will drag Lev's soul
to paradise
bends over him
and shouting above
the hoarse breathing
the terrible noises of the chest
slyly asks
—And what now
—I must run away
says Lev
and repeats once more
—I must run away

—Where to—asks Pimen
—Where to O Christian soul

Lev fell silent
he hid in eternal shadow
eternal silence

no one understood the prophecy
as if the words of Scripture were not known

"nation shall rise against nation
and Kingdom against Kingdom
some shall fall by the sword
and others be chased into slavery
among all the nations
for these will be days of vengeance
so all that is written
will be fulfilled"

so arrives the time
of abandoning homes
of wandering in jungles
of frantic sea voyages
circlings in the darkness
crawling in dust

the time of the hunted

the time of the Great Beast

THE FABLE ABOUT A NAIL

For lack of a nail the kingdom has fallen
—according to the wisdom of nursery schools—but in our
    kingdom
there have been no nails for a long time there aren't and
    won't be
either the small ones for hanging a picture
on a wall or large ones for closing a coffin

but despite this or maybe because of it
the kingdom persists and is even admired by others
how can one live without a nail paper or string
bricks oxygen freedom and whatever else
obviously one can since the kingdom lasts and lasts

people live in homes in our country not in caves
factories smoke on the steppe a train runs through the tundra
and a ship bleats on the cold ocean
there is an army and police an official seal hymn and flag
in appearance everything like anywhere in the world

but only in appearance for our kingdom
is not a creation of nature or a human creation
seemingly permanent built on the bones of mammoths
in reality it is weak as if brought to a stop
between act and thought being and nonbeing

    what is real—a leaf and a stone—falls
    but spectres live long obstinately despite

the rising and setting of the sun revolutions of
    heavenly bodies
on the shamed earth fall the tears of objects

ELEGY FOR THE DEPARTURE OF
PEN INK AND LAMP

I

Truly my betrayal is great and hard to forgive
for I do not remember either the day or hour
when I abandoned you friends of my childhood

first I humbly turn to you
pen with a wooden handle
covered with paint or brittle lacquer

in a Jewish shop
—steps creaking a bell at the glass door—
I chose you
in the color of laziness
and soon afterward you carried
on your body
the reveries of my teeth
traces of school torment

o silver nib
outlet of the critical mind
messenger of soothing knowledge
—that the globe is round
—that parallel lines never meet
in a box of the storekeeper
you were a like a fish waiting for me
in a school of other fish
—I was astonished there were so many
completely mute objects

without owners—
then
mine forever
I put you respectfully in my mouth
and for a long time felt on my tongue
a taste
of sorrel
and the moon

o ink
illustrious Mr. Ink
of distinguished ancestry
highly born
like the sky at evening
for a long time drying
deliberate
and very patient
in wells we transformed you
into the Sargasso Sea
drowning in your wise depths
blotters hair secret oaths and flies
to block out the smell
of a gentle volcano
the call of the abyss

who remembers you today
dear companions
you left quietly
beyond the last cataract of time
who recalls you with gratitude
in the era of fatheaded ball-point pens
arrogant objects

without grace
name
or past

when I speak of you
I would like it to be
as if I were hanging an ex-voto
on a shattered altar

2
Light of my childhood
blessed lamp

sometimes in junk stores
I come upon
your disgraced body

and yet you were once
a bright allegory

a spirit stubbornly battling
the demons of gnosis
wholly given to the eyes

in full sight
transparently simple

at the bottom of the fount
kerosene—elixir of primeval forests
slick snake of a wick
with a blazing head
the slender maiden's chimney

and silvery shield of tin
like Selene a full moon

your moods of a princess
beautiful and cruel

tantrums of a prima donna
not applauded enough

lo
a serene aria
summer's honey-light
above the flue of the chimney
a light braid of good weather

then all of a sudden
dark basses
a raid of crows and ravens
curses and maledictions
prophecy of extermination
fury of sooty smoke

like a great playwright you knew the surf of passions
and swamps of melancholy black towers of pride
glow of fires the rainbow the unleashed sea
effortlessly you could call into being from nothingness
landscapes a savage city repeated in water
at your sign
the mad prince the island and the balcony in Verona
obediently appeared

I was devoted to you
luminous initiation
instrument of knowledge
under the hammers of night

while my flat
second head projected on the ceiling
looked down filled with terror
as if from an angel's loge
at the theater of the world
all entangled
evil
cruel

I thought then
that before the deluge it was necessary
to save
one
thing
small
warm
faithful

so it continues further
with ourselves inside it as in a shell

3
I never believed in the spirit of history
an invented monster with a murderous look
dialectical beast on a leash led by slaughterers

nor in you—four horsemen of the apocalypse
Huns of progress galloping over earthly and heavenly steppes
destroying on the way everything worthy of respect old and
    defenseless

I spent years learning the simplistic cogwheels of history
a monotonous procession hopeless struggle
scoundrels at the head of confused crowds
against the handful of the honest courageous aware

I have
very little left

objects
and compassion

lightheartedly we leave the gardens of childhood gardens of
    things
shedding in flight manuscripts oil-lamps dignity pens
such is our illusory journey at the edge of nothingness

> pen with an ancient nib forgive my unfaithfulness
> and you inkwell—there are still so many good thoughts
>   in you
> forgive me kerosene lamp—you are dying in my memory
>   like a deserted campsite

> I paid for the betrayal
> but I did not know then
> you were leaving forever

> and that it will be
> dark

ZBIGNIEW HERBERT (1924–1998) was a spiritual leader of the anticommunist movement in Poland. His work has been translated into almost every European language and has won numerous prizes, most recently the Jerusalem Prize and the T. S. Eliot Prize. He wrote *Selected Poems, Report from the Besieged City and Other Poems, Mr. Cogito, Still Life with a Bridle,* and most recently *The King of the Ants: Mythological Essays,* all published by The Ecco Press.

JOHN AND BOGDANA CARPENTER, longtime Herbert translators, won the PEN Translation Award for his *Selected Poems.* John Carpenter is a poet and a critic; Bogdana Carpenter is a professor of Slavic Languages and Literature at the University of Michigan. They live in Ann Arbor, Michigan.